25–

W9-BRY-408

RODNEY KING AND THE
L.A. RIOTS

RODNEY KING AND THE
L.A. RIOTS

BY REBECCA RISSMAN

CONTENT CONSULTANT
DARNELL M. HUNT, PHD
DIRECTOR, BUNCHE CENTER AT UCLA
PROFESSOR OF SOCIOLOGY

ABDO
Publishing Company

CREDITS

Published by ABDO Publishing Company, PO Box 398166, Minneapolis, MN 55439. Copyright © 2014 by Abdo Consulting Group, Inc. International copyrights reserved in all countries. No part of this book may be reproduced in any form without written permission from the publisher. The Essential Library™ is a trademark and logo of ABDO Publishing Company.

Printed in the United States of America,
North Mankato, Minnesota
102013
012014

Editor: Melissa York
Series Designer: Becky Daum

Photo credits: Reed Saxon/AP Images, cover, 2, 30, 39; Mark Peterson/Corbis, 6, 90; Mark J. Terrill/AP Images, 9, 57; AP Images, 14, 27, 43, 48; Craig Fujii/AP Images, 18; KTLA Los Angeles, George Holliday/AP Images, 20; Red Line Editorial, 35; Dan Levine/Reuters/Corbis, 40; Steve Grayson/AP Images, 51; Bob Galbraith/Corbis, 59; Nick Ut/AP Images, 60, 78, 83; Paul Sakuma/AP Images, 63; Chris Martinez/AP Images, 65; John Gaps III/AP Images, 68; David Longstreath/AP Images, 71; Ted Soqui/Corbis, 75; Joseph Sohm/Visions of America/Corbis, 86; Mark Sayles/AP Images, 95

Library of Congress Control Number: 2013946965

Cataloging-in-Publication Data

Rissman, Rebecca.
 Rodney King and the L.A. riots / Rebecca Rissman.
  p. cm. -- (Essential events)
Includes bibliographical references and index.
ISBN 978-1-62403-260-8
1. Riots--California--Los Angeles--History--20th century--Juvenile literature. 2. Los Angeles (Calif.)--Race relations--Juvenile literature. 3. Violence--California--Los Angeles--History--20th century--Juvenile literature. 4. Racism--California--Los Angeles--Juvenile literature. 5. King, Rodney, 1965-2012--Juvenile literature. I. Title.
979.4--dc23

2013946965

CONTENTS

CHAPTER
ONE

THE ARREST THAT MADE HISTORY

It was not long after midnight on March 3, 1991. Husband-and-wife California Highway Patrol (CHP) team Tim and Melanie Singer spotted a white car speeding on the 210 Freeway in Los Angeles, California. They followed the car, astonished as it exceeded speeds of 110 miles per hour (177 kmh) on the freeway, and then up to 85 miles per hour (137 kmh) on residential roads.[1] The Singers grew more and more nervous as the car ran red lights and almost caused an accident.

Finally, after a 7.8-mile (12.6 km) chase, the driver came to a stop in a residential neighborhood in Los Angeles. By this point, several Los Angeles Police Department (LAPD) units had arrived on the scene, and an LAPD helicopter hovered overhead. Tim Singer yelled over his loudspeaker for everyone to exit the car. He realized the noise of the helicopter overhead, combined with the sirens of the squad cars, might make

The Los Angeles Police Department had a mixed reputation in the 1990s.

it difficult for the people in the car to understand him. Singer stepped out of his car and yelled again, this time making sure everyone could hear him. The two passengers, Freddie Helms and "Pooh" Allen, followed his orders to exit the vehicle and get on the ground. The driver, however, stayed in the car. While Tim Singer dealt with Helms and Allen, Melanie Singer approached the car and repeated the order to the driver.

Rodney King's Arrest

After a tense few moments, the driver, 25-year-old African-American Rodney King, stepped out of the vehicle. His behavior was odd. Instead of looking scared, he smiled and waved at the hovering helicopter. He was sweating heavily and reached for his pockets more than once, making the law enforcement officials nervous he was reaching for a gun. Finally, King listened to law enforcement and got down on the ground.

Melanie Singer had her gun pointed at King. She was about to handcuff King when LAPD Sergeant Stacey Koon stepped in. He had been watching the Singers try to convince the driver to exit his vehicle. Koon did not want Singer using a weapon in a situation this tense. He later testified he was worried King could overpower

Melanie Singer later testified in court about the events she witnessed that morning.

Singer and take her weapon. Koon told her he and the LAPD would take over the situation.

Sergeant Koon ordered LAPD officers Laurence Powell, Timothy Wind, Theodore Briseno, and Rolando Solano to swarm King. As later court testimony would show, the four officers were young and relatively inexperienced. Powell was 28 years old, with just over three years of experience. He was regarded as hardworking but also hot tempered. Just before the incident on March 3, Powell had been singled out for needing to improve his technique using his police baton. Former Green Beret Wind, at 30 years old, was more mature. Briseno, at 38 years old, was the oldest officer involved. He had a mixed record with some awards for excellence at work but also a suspension for the use of excessive force on a suspect. The last officer ordered to swarm King was 27-year-old Solano. A rookie with only five months of experience, Solano was hardly prepared to deal with the incident unfolding before him.

LAPD: HEROES OR VILLAINS OF LOS ANGELES?

At the time of the King assault, many people had mixed feelings about the LAPD. The popular television show Dragnet had portrayed the police force as smart, balanced, and capable. The LAPD had a long history of recruiting only the most qualified police. Many people in Los Angeles still believed in this ideal. When Officer Wind applied to work for the LAPD, he said he "wanted to be with the best."[2]

However, Los Angeles was growing and changing. During the second half of the 1900s, racial tensions in the city started increasing. Large numbers of African-American, Asian, and Latino people migrated into the city. At the same time, complaints started arising about police abusing their authority. Others worried the officers were acting on racist beliefs. Police struggled to maintain order.

King Fights Back

The four LAPD officers held down King and attempted to handcuff him. However, King managed to throw off the men and even struck Briseno in the chest. The officers were amazed; one man had somehow overpowered four trained police officers. Briseno later remembered wondering, "I don't know what's going on . . . but I'm thinking, man, this sucker is on something."[3] The LAPD officers started suspecting King was using PCP, a powerful street drug that often makes its users feel invulnerable and do risky things. However, drug tests later revealed King had not used PCP.

Koon ordered his officers to back off of King. He, too, later testified he was concerned King was using PCP. He knew the drug made it almost impossible

PCP

PCP is an illegal street drug that was commonly abused in Los Angeles in the 1980s and 1990s. It often causes people to become aggressive and unreasonable, and it can cause people to have difficulty understanding what is happening around them. LAPD officers familiar with PCP often reported it gave users huge bursts of strength and power. The users were not actually stronger than normal, but they lost fear and a sense of their own limits, allowing for unusual surges of action. PCP users were regarded as extremely dangerous to arresting officers. King's blood tests after his arrest would show he did not in fact have PCP in his system at the time of his assault.

to overpower its users with simple police maneuvers. The mistaken impression King was using this drug heightened the tension on the scene. Officer Solano quickly stood back with the other police bystanders. He later said he was terrified.

Koon decided he needed to take down the suspect with a stronger tool, a police Taser. This weapon delivers a powerful electric shock that briefly disables the target. Koon used his Taser on King once, hitting him in the back. The electric shock made King groan and fall to the ground. It looked as though the police had finally gained the upper hand with the suspect. But suddenly, King stood up again. Koon could hardly believe it. He warned the LAPD to stay back and used his Taser again, this time hitting King in the chest. King stumbled but again managed to stand up. Koon decided to step things up. The sergeant ordered officers Powell and Wind to subdue the suspect using their batons.

It was during this tense moment that George Holliday, a neighbor who had been disturbed by the police commotion below his apartment, began filming the incident from his balcony on his new video recorder. No one on the street knew they were being observed or filmed.

Powell and Wind walked toward King, prepared to deliver power strokes, or forceful blows, to King's joints with their police batons. King lunged directly at Powell. The officer raised his arm and swung his baton strongly down. Witnesses to the event disagree whether he struck King in the head, but King was thrown to the ground. When he rose again, King's face was bloodied and his cheekbone had been shattered.

> ## LAPD BATONS
>
> Police batons are long, thick metal rods. They are usually used to intimidate suspects, but they are occasionally used as weapons. In extreme cases, police hit suspects with their batons in a power stroke. When performed correctly, this maneuver can disable suspects quickly with as little injury as possible. Police can then safely handcuff the suspects without worrying they will try to fight.

Over the next 81 seconds, as recorded in Holliday's video, Powell and Wind struck King approximately 56 times with their batons and delivered several strong kicks.[4] Officer Briseno stepped in once to stomp on King's back. Sergeant Koon stood by, watching the entire incident. He later reflected he had ordered his officers to "hit [King's] joints, hit the wrists, hit his elbows, hit his knees, hit his ankles."[5] However, the injuries King suffered showed many of the baton blows were to his head, back, and torso. By the time King was

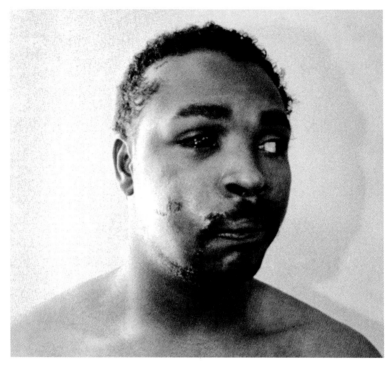

Rodney King was seriously injured by the police. This photo was taken three days after the beating.

finally handcuffed, he had suffered a broken ankle, a broken cheekbone, and countless bruises.

Calling an Ambulance

In the moments after King was finally handcuffed, Officer Powell called for an ambulance. When the police operator asked him what it was for, Powell responded, "A victim of ah, ah . . . beating." Powell then laughed and continued, saying "Yeah . . . numerous head wounds." He then messaged LAPD Officer Corina Smith using the digital messaging system in his squad car:

Powell: Oops

Smith: Oops what?

Powell: I haven't beaten anyone this bad in a long time.

Smith: Oh, not again. Why [did] you do that? I thought you agreed to chill out for a while. What did he do?

Powell: I think he was dusted . . . many broken bones later.[6]

Powell's excessive use of force, as well as his casual attitude about the incident, would soon come to haunt him. Sergeant Koon, on the other hand, believed his team of officers had behaved appropriately. Immediately after the beating, Koon reported the incident to headquarters. He noted there had been a "big time use of force" but did not report any extra details about it.[7]

SERGEANT KOON

Stacey Koon was a well-respected police sergeant in Los Angeles. He had received more than 90 commendations, or police awards, for his excellence in service. He had also pushed to discipline a white LAPD officer for using excessive force against two homeless African-American men. He believed strongly in the policies and practices of the LAPD. After the King assault, Koon defended the actions taken by the LAPD that night. However, a federal jury did not agree. Koon was charged with violating King's civil rights, found guilty, and served prison time.

What King, Koon, Powell, and the others did not know was they would all become famous very soon. Holliday was still standing on his balcony, wondering what to do with the extremely graphic videotape he'd just recorded.

A Question of Race

In addition to questioning the extent of King's beating, many would later wonder if the LAPD officers' actions were based on King's race. It was hard to ignore the facts: a group of white police officers had brutally assaulted an unarmed African-American man. Some people feared this incident was a reflection of widespread racism in the mostly white LAPD.

In 1990, just before King's assault, the *Los Angeles Times* conducted a poll of residents of Southern California that showed African Americans had growing concerns about racism, discrimination, and prejudice in the LAPD. Nearly half the African-American responders complained about police brutality, and one-fifth said they had "no confidence" they could trust the police to protect them from crime.[9] These numbers were far higher than those reported by white responders. African Americans in Los Angeles were growing fearful of—and frustrated with—the LAPD. These feelings would soon boil over in one of the largest riots the United States had ever seen.

CHAPTER
TWO

AN EARLY VIRAL VIDEO

Shortly after midnight on March 3, 1991, the sounds of police sirens, a hovering helicopter, and angry shouts woke George Holliday from a deep sleep. He walked to his balcony and spotted a group of police officers involved in a physical scuffle with an African-American man on the street below. Knowing the scene below his apartment was odd, Holliday began filming on his new Sony camcorder.

Holliday wasn't the only person trying to film the incident. In fact, two of his neighbors also tried to record the violent scene. However, only Holliday was able to start filming in time to capture the majority of King's beating.

The video Holliday recorded that night wasn't perfect. It was grainy and lost focus at one point. His balcony was approximately 90 feet (27 m) away from the incident. He had to zoom in to see the participants,

George Holliday was in the right place at the right time to capture the incident on tape.

Holliday's video shows police officers beating King on the ground.

which reduced the clarity of his video. Despite this, the 81 seconds of film he managed to capture that night would change history. Of course, he did not know that at the time. After the commotion died down, Holliday went back to bed.

Holliday Shares His Film

Later that morning, Holliday thought about his recorded video. He was sure someone in the police department should see it. He tried calling the LAPD, but he remembered being "pretty much hung up" on.[1] Next, he tried calling cable news network CNN. Again, his calls were ignored. The following Monday, March 4, he showed the video to his local news station, KTLA. Finally someone listened. The station gladly accepted the tape, stunned by its violent footage. The station's news director remembered, "We were all shocked by [the tape] and knew from the first that it was important."[2]

The same day, an employee of KTLA delivered a copy of the tape to LAPD headquarters. The news station suspected the police would want to know what the nation was about to see. The tape shocked the police. Captain Tim McBride later remarked he knew the video was going to have a huge impact on the police force: "Anybody who would look at it . . . would want to do an investigation."[3]

The LAPD Reacts to the Tape

The LAPD immediately ordered Internal Affairs officers to start examining the incident. They wanted to know which officers were involved, why force had been used, and what started the incident. Investigators quickly started work, knowing they would have many angry people to deal with when the footage hit the news. The news stations acted quickly on their new sensational piece of tape. The LAPD investigators had not even finished identifying the officers on the tape when the video played on that evening's news.

KTLA edited Holliday's tape to omit some blurry footage and aired the new, edited, 68-second version at 10:15 p.m. on March 4.[4] It caused an immediate impact. Suddenly, it seemed as though Holliday's grainy home film was all people were talking about. KTLA passed the video to other news stations around the world. The clip was shown so often an executive at CNN remarked,

IMPORTANCE OF EDITS

The original tape Holliday submitted to KTLA shows 81 seconds of King and the LAPD. The tape begins with a three-second shot of King charging Powell, who responds with a baton blow that knocks down King. Then the tape goes blurry for ten seconds as Holliday adjusts his view. When the tape refocuses, it clearly shows the LAPD violently beating King.

When KTLA aired the video, the news station edited the film for clarity. Their edits removed the ten seconds of blurry footage as well as the three-second segment showing King running at Powell. The LAPD's defense team would later argue that element of the tape was crucial. Without it, it seemed as though the LAPD officers had attacked King for no reason. If viewers had seen the clip in its entirety, they might have interpreted the LAPD officers as responding to a violent or unstable suspect.

The news stations that aired the footage around the nation did not know the clip had been edited. They believed they were showing the entire video in their newscasts. Networks later began airing the unedited version of the film, but for many people, the edited version became the iconic image of the event they remembered. They still felt the tape showed the LAPD using excessive force.

"Television used the tape like wallpaper."[5] Made long before the age of YouTube, it was one of the country's first viral videos. It played so often it became a cultural phenomenon.

LAPD Chief Daryl Gates was in Washington, DC, during the incident. He did not see the tape until he returned to Los Angeles around midnight on March 4. He remembered watching the tape 25 times. As he later reflected,

> To see my officers engaged in what appeared to be excessive use of force, possibly criminally excessive, to see them beat a man with their batons fifty-six times, to see a sergeant on scene who did nothing to seize control, was something I never dreamed I would witness.[6]

Captain Paul Jefferson, an African-American LAPD officer, remembered watching the footage on the

MORE AIRTIME THAN THE PERSIAN GULF WAR

Holliday filmed the Rodney King beating on the same day Iraq accepted the terms of the United States and its allies that ended the Persian Gulf War. The war had begun in 1990 and focused on Iraq's invasion of Kuwait. Most Americans had followed the footage closely on news stations including CNN. When Holliday's footage hit the airwaves, it quickly eclipsed the end of the war in terms of social impact and airtime. News reporters recognized that race continued to be a preeminent issue in American society, arguably more immediate and pressing to most Americans than what was happening in the Persian Gulf.

evening news while in the Van Nuys Police Station in Los Angeles. As were many African-American LAPD officers, Jefferson was well aware of the police force's reputation for using excessive force against minorities. However, he was still shocked to see the tape. "It was unreal," he said. "When the [other] officers saw the tape, there wasn't a word said. They just turned around and walked out with their heads down. Nobody said a word. They were in shock."[7] While the video sent shock waves through the LAPD, it was also stunning news viewers around the world.

The World Sees the Video

By March 6, Holliday's video had spread like wildfire. Networks NBC, CNN, CBS, and ABC were all airing the

IF IT HADN'T BEEN FILMED

As the King beating "wallpapered" television screens around the world, many viewers wondered how many similar beatings had occurred that weren't filmed. The presence of Holliday's video did not just shed light on one violent arrest. It made people suspicious that similar, unrecorded events had been happening all around them. Complaints about police discrimination, prejudice, and racism had already begun plaguing the LAPD. The Holliday tape simply made the problem more obvious for many. Instead of looking to law enforcement officials as community leaders and trustworthy resources, more and more people in minority communities began seeing police officers as potentially violent bullies.

footage on local and national news programs. In Los Angeles, especially, the tape seemed to take over the airwaves. People, especially whites, were shocked to watch what looked like three LAPD officers violently beating a man while another LAPD supervisor stood nearby and watched. However, many blacks and Latinos felt the Holliday video finally exposed the abuses they had known about for years.

Later that day, King was released from the Los Angeles County Men's Central Jail without charges. A district attorney said King was released because prosecutors did not have enough evidence against him. He had not tested positive for PCP, but his blood alcohol showed he had been drinking and driving. This offense was not serious enough to continue holding King in jail. A famous photo taken that day shows King looking swollen and bruised, with a bloodied eye. The image, along with the repeatedly aired footage of the beating, made it seem as though the LAPD had beaten an innocent man for no reason. The American Civil Liberties Union ran a full-page advertisement in the *Los Angeles Times* on March 12 that read: "Who do you call when the gang wears blue uniforms?"[8]

Residents of Los Angeles React

Residents of Los Angeles reacted to the incident with disbelief and anger. A poll taken by the *Los Angeles Times* showed 86 percent of the people surveyed had seen the video. This large percentage showed how much airtime the video had been given on different news stations. The poll also showed 92 percent of the people who had seen the video believed it showed excessive force.[9] This meant viewers felt the officers had used more violence than was necessary to subdue King.

African Americans living in Los Angeles responded with more anger than other communities. In the 1980s and 1990s, many L.A. African Americans felt resentful toward the LAPD. They worried they were being unfairly targeted by law enforcement. They also felt as though law enforcement did not protect them as

Controversy immediately surrounded LAPD Chief Gates after footage of the beating appeared in the media.

much as it protected other groups in the area. Many felt Holliday's film finally revealed to the rest of the world just how unfairly African Americans were treated by law enforcement in Los Angeles.

Gates knew the tape could make his police department seem corrupt and dangerous. He was worried about the impact it could have on the future of the LAPD. Gates wrote later the film showed "a very, very extreme use of force—extreme for any police department in America. But for the LAPD, considered by many to be perhaps the finest, most professional police department in the world, it was more than extreme. It was impossible."[11] As soon as the LAPD identified the officers involved in the incident, it suspended them. This meant they were required to turn in their badges and firearms and could not return to work. Police Chief Gates announced his belief the officers involved in the incident should be prosecuted. L.A. mayor Tom Bradley added his opinion, saying, "This is something that we cannot and will not tolerate."[13]

The efforts made by law enforcement and government officials to publicly condemn the actions of the LAPD did not make L.A. residents feel better about the incident. Instead, they fueled the already-boiling anger of a frustrated community. Minorities living in Los Angeles had become accustomed to the idea the LAPD was not there to protect them. Instead, they believed the LAPD was there to harass, discriminate against, and unfairly arrest them. The overwhelming perception among some communities was that the LAPD did not value minority life. The King beating was simply a well-publicized incident that reflected a larger problem for minorities in the city. It was proof of a problem many had complained about for years. As journalist Lou Cannon later noted in his book about the riots, it was "almost impossible to turn on a television set without seeing a clip from the Holliday tape or an outraged public official demanding prosecution of the 'white officers who had beaten a black motorist.'"[14] It was becoming clear Los Angeles was an unstable, angry city. But no one could have guessed how dangerous that anger was becoming.

CHAPTER
THREE

LIFE IN LOS ANGELES

In 1990, Los Angeles was an extremely diverse city. Slightly more than half of the population identified as white. The other half was made up of Latinos, Asians, African Americans, and other races.[1] This diversity was reflected in the 106 languages spoken by L.A. residents. Nearly half of public schoolchildren spoke Spanish at home.[2] To many, Los Angeles was a great example of the American melting pot of diversity.

Tom Bradley, the first African-American mayor of Los Angeles, had run the city since 1973. Mayor Bradley was proud to have led the city during a time of exciting economic growth. In the 1970s and 1980s, the US government spent huge amounts of money on military and defense facilities located in Los Angeles. This provided the residents of the city with jobs and money. People moved to the city from all over the world. Mayor Bradley even successfully campaigned for Los Angeles

Tom Bradley was the leader of a large and diverse city at the start of the 1990s.

to host the 1984 Olympic games. It seemed as though Los Angeles, often called "the city of dreams," was an ideal place to live and work.

In the late 1980s and early 1990s, however, the state of California suffered a huge economic crash. The government stopped spending as much money on military defense. Much of California's workforce was employed by military defense companies. Factories that produced airplanes, bombs, and other weapons fired thousands of employees. From 1988 to 1993, California lost 140,000 jobs in the aerospace industry alone.[3] Even residents who did not work in this industry suffered. The more money the city lost, the harder it became for residents to support small neighborhood businesses that were often run by less educated and lower-paid residents.

Despite the economic hardships, however, California's population continued growing.

Tensions in South Central

Racial tensions were growing in South Central, an economically disadvantaged L.A. neighborhood known today as South L.A. Ninety-two percent of South Central's residents were African American or Latino, and more than 35 percent of them lived below the poverty line.[5] A shocking 13 percent were unemployed.[6] The high percentages of unemployed minorities seemed to contrast with the city's white residents. A racial divide was forming in Los Angeles. White residents were more likely to be well educated, hold jobs, and live in safe neighborhoods. Minority residents, on the other hand, generally had lower levels of education and were often unable to find work. They tended to live in neighborhoods that were growing more and more unsafe.

Violent crime in Los Angeles was an increasing problem in the late 1980s and early 1990s. African Americans, especially those who lived in high-crime and low-income neighborhoods including South Central, reported that violent crime and the fear it caused was the worst part of life in Southern California. A surge in the use of crack cocaine, an addictive and illegal street drug, increased the incidence of violent crime around Los Angeles.

Operation Hammer

Chief Gates tried to take action to stem the violent crime in the city. In April 1988, he introduced Operation Hammer, a police program that attempted to stop crimes before they were committed. As part of Operation Hammer, as many as 1,000 police officers moved from neighborhood to neighborhood, arresting suspected drug dealers and gang members. Chief Gates felt this would send a message to criminals in the city that the police were cracking down. Instead, the rate of violent crime continued rising.

Operation Hammer did successfully take many gang members and drug dealers off the streets. However, it accomplished this by routinely rounding up law-abiding African-American residents for questioning.

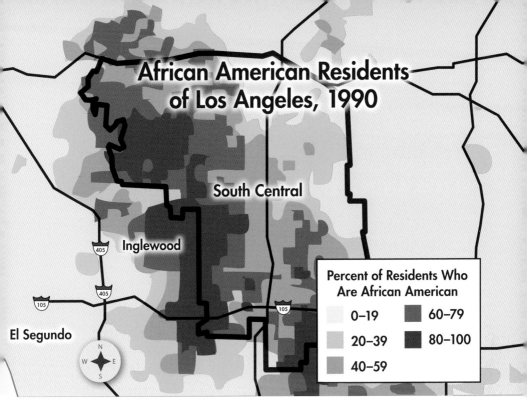

African American Residents of Los Angeles, 1990

South Central

405 Inglewood

405

105

El Segundo

N
W · E
S

Percent of Residents Who Are African American

	0–19		60–79
	20–39		80–100
	40–59		

Occasionally, this questioning turned physical. Operation Hammer specifically targeted young male African Americans. They complained of being stopped by the police just because they were in the wrong place at the wrong time. They were often "proned out," or made to lie facedown on the ground so they could be searched. This was humiliating. Many began feeling as though LAPD officers were abusing their power.

Prejudices and Discrimination

Tension brewed between African Americans in South Central and the LAPD. African Americans felt as though they were being singled out as the cause of the violence and poverty in Los Angeles. They did not want to be abused by the police. The LAPD, on the other hand, struggled to maintain peace and order in a diverse and increasingly dangerous city. While some officers were guilty of singling out and discriminating against African Americans, the vast majority of the LAPD worked toward the equal and fair treatment of all residents.

The friction between the LAPD and African-American residents was not the only cause of tension in the city in the late 1980s. The Korean-American population also struggled with prejudice from white, Latino, and African-American residents. *LA Times* journalist Edward Chang remembered there was a "three-tiered system" in the city: "whites on top, Latinos and blacks at the bottom" with relatively little power to oppress other groups, and

"Asians in between."[8] Many Korean Americans owned small stores and businesses in South Central. But they were isolated. Other racial groups did not engage with them. Hostility developed between African Americans and Korean Americans based on stereotypes each group believed about the other.

THIRTY-NINTH AND DALTON

On August 1, 1988, the LAPD raided four apartments on the corner of Thirty-Ninth Street and Dalton Avenue in Los Angeles as part of Operation Hammer. They were responding to a tip that the apartments were being used to sell and store crack cocaine. More than 80 officers stormed the apartments, destroying furniture, smashing toilets, breaking windows, and even writing pro-police graffiti on an outside wall.

Residents of the apartment complex complained the police used unnecessary force in their raid. Tammy Moore, a resident, reported the police knocked her seven-month-old son from her arms as they rushed into the building. Another resident reported he was struck in the face by an officer's flashlight.

Police arrested 33 African Americans in the raid. However, it seemed as though the tip had been wrong. The entire raid collected less than one ounce (28g) of cocaine and six ounces (170g) of marijuana. It was far less than the police had believed they would discover.

This raid was a huge embarrassment for the LAPD. Many of the officers involved were disciplined for their poor behavior, and three were prosecuted on felony vandalism charges. LAPD commander Chet Spencer remarked it was "an extremely dark day in the history of the Los Angeles Police Department."[9] The raid made the LAPD appear unprofessional, cruel, and unnecessarily violent.

LATASHA HARLINS

On March 16, 1991, 15-year-old African-American student Latasha Harlins tried to buy an orange juice at a Los Angeles liquor store. After an argument with the cashier, Korean-American Soon Ja Du, Harlins left the orange juice and tried to exit the store. Du believed she was trying to steal, and she shot her in the back of the head, killing her. Du was convicted of voluntary manslaughter and sentenced to five years of probation. The conviction of manslaughter acknowledged the killing was illegal but did not place as much blame on Du as a charge of murder would have. Many Americans felt Du's punishment was not equal to her crime. They felt she should have been charged with a greater crime and made to serve time in prison for her actions.

By the time of the Rodney King beating, life in Los Angeles had grown difficult for many people. Racial tensions had reached a breaking point. Economic struggles had led to large groups of minorities living in desperately poor conditions. White residents of Los Angeles appeared to enjoy a far greater quality of life than their minority counterparts. This divide was becoming more and more obvious with each passing year. What had once been called "the city of dreams" had become an unstable and violent place to live. Law enforcement officials, government leaders, and residents alike could tell the city needed help. But no one could have predicted what was about to happen.

Poverty and violence plagued many neighborhoods
in Los Angeles in the 1990s.

CHAPTER
FOUR

WHO IS RODNEY KING?

R odney Glen King was born on April 4, 1965, in Sacramento, California. He lived with his four siblings, his mother, Odessa King, and his father, Ronald King. His father was an abusive alcoholic who struggled to keep a steady job. His mother was a member of the Jehovah's Witnesses religious group, and she often worried about her husband's alcoholism.

When Rodney was young, his family moved to Altadena, a neighborhood in Los Angeles, because his father felt he would have a better chance of finding work there. When he was sober, Ronald worked off and on in construction and janitorial jobs. This work was occasionally hard to find, and the King family sometimes had trouble putting enough food on the table.

Some of Rodney's fondest childhood memories involved fishing with his father. They both loved spending time together at rivers and creeks and could

Rodney King faced many challenges in his life before and after the beating.

spend hours catching fish for dinner. However, it was during an afternoon fishing trip that Rodney first encountered the racism that would later change his life.

While fishing with his brothers one sunny day, Rodney briefly hopped into the water for a swim. While he was in the water, a group of white children began throwing rocks at him. The white children chased him

WATTS RIOT

Four months after Rodney King was born, a historic riot erupted in a poor African-American neighborhood of Los Angeles. On August 11, 1965, an African-American motorist, Marquette Frye, was pulled over by a white CHP officer, Lee W. Minikus. A crowd witnessed Minikus arrest Frye, whom he suspected of driving drunk. The tensions between the crowd and the police grew until the crowd grew violent. Soon, the neighborhood was engulfed in a riot.

For six days, the South Central neighborhood was ruled by chaos and violence. Rioters overturned cars, damaged stores, and set fires. Eventually, more than 14,000 California National Guard troops were sent in to control the crowds.

By the time the riot had calmed down, 34 people had been killed, more than 1,000 were wounded, and nearly 4,000 had been arrested.[1]

While the riot raged, law enforcement and city officials blamed it on troublemakers from outside the community. However, after the violence subsided, Governor Pat Brown ordered an investigation into the causes of the riot. The investigation discovered the riot stemmed from community dissatisfaction with unemployment, poor housing, and bad schools. The Watts riot brought attention to the poor quality of life faced by African Americans living in Los Angeles. Unfortunately, throughout the time King lived in the city, little changed to improve the area.

The racial tensions that had erupted into violence in 1965 were still an issue as Rodney grew up.

out of the water, calling him racist names. Rodney's two brothers were also targeted that day. One brother told Rodney, "They wanted to kill us. That big redhead was gonna tie me up with a rope he had wrapped around a big rock. . . . He was screaming he was gonna kill us, but we took off before his friends could catch us."[2] In the years after the incident, Rodney realized he and his brothers were targeted because of their race: "It turned out that because we had different hair and darker skin, the kids with lighter skin didn't like playing with us."[3] This incident was the first time Rodney encountered racism.

A Difficult Childhood

Rodney's childhood was not easy. In addition to having a drinking problem, Rodney's father also physically abused his wife and children. In the years after his assault, Rodney King commented on his father's beatings, noting "maybe those whuppings prepared me for Koon."[4]

From fourth to sixth grade, Rodney earned money by working alongside his father as a night-shift janitor from 5:00 p.m. until 2:00 a.m. Then he would go home for a few hours of sleep before school started. Rodney knew working nights hurt his performance in school. His teachers worried he could hardly read, and his memory was poor. It became clear he had a learning disability. Rodney's teachers assigned him to special classes, but he dropped out of high school to take a construction job just six months before graduation.

Trouble with the Law

In 1982, as a teen, King fathered his first child with his girlfriend, Carmen Simpson. Two years later, he

married a different woman,
Denetta Lyles, and had another
child. On July 27, 1987, Lyles
filed a legal claim that King had
beaten her. King did not protest
and was placed on probation
and ordered to get counseling.
He never did so, however. Lyles
and King soon divorced. Later,
King married another woman,
Crystal Waters.

On November 3, 1989,
King was arrested for robbing
a convenience store with a tire
iron. He entered the store and
tried to buy a pack of gum

VALUING EDUCATION

Although King dropped out of school just before graduating, he still valued his education. He worked with a tutor and eventually earned his general equivalency diploma (GED). He also formed a relationship with a political science professor at California Polytechnic State University. In the years after King's beating, the two met often to discuss legal issues, and the professor even invited King to visit the university and address his students.

with food stamps. After the cashier refused him, King
became angry. The two got into a scuffle and King fled
the store with $200 he had taken from the register. King
was quickly found and arrested. He was sentenced to
two years in a state prison for his crime. His probation
officer reflected, "The problem this defendant may
present to the community is not that he steals and

robs but that he may have an explosive temper."[5] This statement would prove to be accurate later in King's life.

In 1990, King was paroled. He reconnected with Waters and promptly found a job on a construction site at Dodger Stadium. He enjoyed his work and social life. It seemed as though he was ready to start fresh. However, the alcoholism that had plagued his father was also becoming a part of King's life.

Drinking and Driving

Part of King's parole was a rule stating that he needed to abstain from alcohol. Despite this, he began drinking heavily. King knew he had a problem with alcohol but was unable to control himself. His favorite drink at the time was a 40-ounce (1.2 L) bottle of beer. On the night he was pulled over and beaten, he had been drinking several of these with his friends while watching a basketball game.

After the basketball game ended, King invited his friends to join him for the car ride. King knew he was being reckless when he got behind the wheel that night. He later reflected,

> I know drinking and driving is not OK . . . and there's no excuse for it. But I had a job to go to that Monday, and

so I went over to a friend's house and popped a couple of beers. We were just sitting around awhile, and I decided to go to a spot where my dad used to take us fishing called Hansen Dam in California.[6]

When he saw the police lights in his rearview mirror, King panicked. He knew getting a DUI would mean going back to prison. He did the only thing he could think of at the time and fled. "I was scared of going back to prison," King said, "and I just kind of thought the problem would just go away."[7] The problem did not just go away, however. The beating he was about to experience would soon force him and his family into the limelight.

KING'S DAUGHTERS

King had three daughters. Candice King was eight years old when her father was beaten. She recalled seeing her father's assault on television: "I was just a kid, but I still saw what was going on," she said. "I was confused and sad— it was my dad." Another of King's daughters, Lora King, was seven years old at the time. She remembered seeing her father days after his beating. "He told me sometimes people won't like you because of your skin color."[8] All of King's children and family members were strongly affected by his beating.

L.A. CO. DISTRICT ATTY.

NAME
DOB
CASE
DATE

L.A. CO. DISTRICT ATTY.

NAME LAURENCE POWELL
DOB
CASE
DATE

L.A. CO. DISTRICT ATTY.

NAME
DOB
CASE
DATE

L.A. CO. DISTRICT ATTY.

NAME BRISENO TED
DOB
CASE
DATE

CHAPTER
FIVE

THE SIMI VALLEY TRIAL

Soon after Holliday's videotape shocked television viewers everywhere, Americans began demanding justice. They wanted the four LAPD officers seen on the video to be punished. The public fiercely criticized Laurence Powell, Timothy Wind, Theodore Briseno, and Stacey Koon. On March 8, 1991, L.A. district attorney Ira Reiner announced he would seek indictments against the officers from a grand jury. If indictments were issued, the four officers would be formally charged with assault with a deadly weapon and use of excessive force. On March 14, the grand jury returned indictments against all the officers. Most Americans welcomed this news because it seemed as though a trial would shed light on why the King beating had occurred. It would also ensure the guilty parties were punished.

Clockwise from top left, officers Wind, Powell, Briseno, and Koon were charged in the King beating.

From L.A. to Simi Valley

The trial was set to take place in Los Angeles County, the county in which the beating had occurred. Each of the defense lawyers representing the four officers fought hard to have the trial moved to a different location. They knew the presence of the media, angry locals, and the tense environment in Los Angeles would make it difficult to have a fair trial. They feared the community's anger toward the LAPD would negatively influence the jury. Judge Bernard Kamins denied the first requests to have the trial moved out of the area.

However, a scandal soon rocked the trial when it was discovered Judge Kamins had been inappropriately communicating with the prosecution lawyers, who represented King. When it appeared as though another attempt to move the trial out of Los Angeles might occur, Kamins wrote a message to the prosecution saying, "Don't panic. You can trust me."[1] The defense felt this message showed Kamins was biased and favored the prosecution. It also showed he was participating in ex parte, or one-sided, communication with the prosecution. This is illegal because it gives one side of

Judge Stanley Weisberg, seen here in 1995,
presided over the Simi Valley trial.

a trial an unfair advantage. Judge Kamins was removed
from the case on August 22, 1991.

After the removal of Kamins, a new judge was
appointed to the trial. On November 26, Judge
Stanley Weisberg allowed the trial to be moved out
of Los Angeles to nearby Simi Valley. This move was
a huge blow to the prosecution's case. Not only did it
remove the jurors from the heated environment of Los
Angeles, in which passionate protesters and frenzied
media generated pressure to find the LAPD officers
guilty, but it also moved the trial into an extremely

RESIDENTIAL SEGREGATION

Los Angeles was a diverse city at the time of the trial. However, the diversity was not evenly distributed throughout the city's many neighborhoods. Rather, many areas were mostly composed of minorities such as African Americans, Asians, and Latinos. Few white people lived in these areas. On the other hand, there were also many white communities in which few minorities lived. White communities clustered in suburbs to the west and north of the city. Latino communities were found mostly in East and South Los Angeles, with African-American communities in South L.A.

conservative city with very different values. Simi Valley was a mostly white community, with only 1.5 percent of its population consisting of African Americans.[2] It was also home to thousands of law enforcement officers and their families.

The move to Simi Valley shocked residents of Los Angeles. Judge Weisberg claimed the new site would be more removed from the media and "convenient" for all parties involved.[3] Most observers, however, saw the change of location as a victory for the defense. Moving the trial from the racially diverse environment of Los Angeles to a mostly white community in which many residents worked in law enforcement made the jury more likely to side with the defense. One leader from the National Association for the Advancement of Colored People (NAACP) reacted to the news, saying,

"It concerns me that we're going to have a criminal jury selected from a community where everybody . . . is either a police officer or is a friend of or related to a police officer."[4] The defense reacted to the news of the location change mildly, saying holding the trial in Simi Valley would simply give both sides "a level playing field."[5]

Soon, the jury selections for the trial brought even more criticism. Many of the jurors seemed to share similar experiences and perspectives. This could make it hard for them to relate to all sides of the trial. Deputy District Attorney Terry White, an African-American man, reacted to the jury selection, saying, "Everyone seemed to be very conservative, very law enforcement oriented, very pro police. . . . They all seemed to come from the same background."[6] The jury selection appeared to favor the defense because it seemed as though

RACE AND JURY

The Simi Valley jury included ten white people, one Hispanic person, and one Asian person. This breakdown was representative of the racial breakdown of Simi Valley but not Los Angeles. Many people worried the predominantly white jury would not be able to relate to the issues addressed at the trial. It was especially troubling to the prosecution that there were no African Americans on the jury.

most members would be more sympathetic to the LAPD than to King.

An Issue of Race?

Before the trial began, few in law enforcement and the legal community felt race had been a primary factor in King's beating. Rather, their general feeling was that it was just a case of an arrest that had gone very wrong. King's own lawyer, Steven Lerman, felt the LAPD officers' actions were in response to his client resisting arrest, not to his race. However, that opinion soon changed as details about one officer emerged.

Officer Powell had a reputation for being brutal and unkind. A fellow officer noted, "He treated everybody like crap. He always had his hand on his gun."[7] Powell was also known for discriminating against African Americans. He had been known to curse at African-American motorists simply for driving in white neighborhoods.

Powell's racist attitudes became a focal point of the trial when the digital messaging system in his squad car was examined. Shortly before the King arrest, Powell received a message from Officer Corina Smith about an arrest. Powell responded, "Sounds almost as exciting as our last call. . . . It was right out of gorillas in the mist."[8] He was referring to a disturbance at an African-American party to which he and Wind had responded. *Gorillas in the Mist* is a film about a naturalist studying gorillas. Powell's comment equated African Americans with gorillas, which sent a clear message about his racial prejudices. With this revelation, the King trial suddenly took on new importance. It was now clearly a trial about racism.

The Trial

On March 26, 1991, all four officers had entered pleas of not guilty in the trial. The officers were still suspended when, almost a year later, on March 5, 1992, the trial began. The defense used the entire

ATTACKING POWELL

Powell's "gorillas in the mist" comment was a big focus of the Simi Valley trial. One of King's lawyers, Terry White, questioned Powell at length about his comment:

> White: Now this call that involved these African Americans, was it in a jungle?
>
> Powell: In a what?
>
> White: A jungle?
>
> Powell: No.
>
> White: Was it at the zoo?
>
> Powell: No.
>
> White: Were there any gorillas around?
>
> Powell: I didn't see any.[9]

White was making it obvious Powell had meant his comment in a racially insensitive way. His line of questioning emphasized how inappropriate Powell had been to use this phrase.

video of the King beating, including the often-omitted three-second segment showing King advancing toward Powell. The defense used two strategies. First, they tried blaming King for the beating, making it look as though his actions were dangerous to the LAPD. Second, they tried pinning the blame on Officer Powell, saying he was "out of control."[10]

Sergeant Koon took the stand, defending himself and explaining his fears about King using PCP. He told the jury he had been frightened by King and had tried to follow police protocol as closely as possible. Susan Clemmer, an LAPD officer who was at the scene during King's beating, took the stand to reinforce this notion.

WHY DIDN'T KING TESTIFY?

King did not testify at the Simi Valley trial. Because he was intoxicated at the time of his arrest, his lawyers worried he might not remember all of the details necessary for an accurate testimony. If he was seen forgetting details or making mistakes on the stand, it might weaken his case.

King had also had previous criminal offenses. Taking the stand would allow the defense to question him about his past, which could also hurt the jury's impression of his character. The prosecution wanted to make sure the jury was sympathetic to King. This would be hard to do if they were associating him with his previous crimes.

Finally, prosecutors kept King from taking the stand because they were afraid he might lose his temper. Any inappropriate behavior or displays of aggression would make the jury feel sympathetic to the LAPD, which would hurt the prosecution's case.

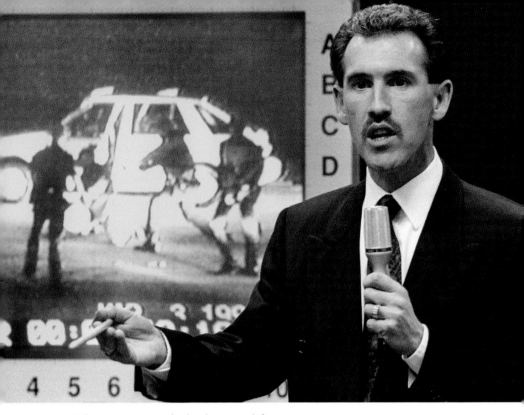

Officer Briseno testified in his own defense.

She testified Powell had told her he was afraid of King
and his incredible strength. Additionally, the defense
called an expert witness to the stand. Sergeant Charles
Duke testified the officers had acted appropriately and
according to police policy.

The prosecution relied on CHP officer Melanie
Singer. She testified she had witnessed Officer Powell
strike King in the face at the beginning of the arrest.
When asked if she could see any reason for the strike,
Melanie Singer responded, "In my opinion, no sir, there
was no reason for it."[11] The prosecution also focused on

Powell's statements after the beating. Two emergency nurses testified they had overheard a conversation between Powell and King at the hospital in which Powell had compared the beating to baseball, calling it "a good hardball game."[12] To many, it seemed as though the prosecution would easily win its case. The evidence, testimonies, and assurance of both the prosecution and the media surrounding the case gave most Americans confidence the four LAPD officers would be found guilty.

After seven days of deliberation, the jury made its decision. At 3:15 p.m. on April 29, 1992, the jury's verdict was announced: all four officers were acquitted. This meant they were found not guilty of using excessive force or assault with a deadly weapon. Just over one hour later, the city of Los Angeles erupted into a massive, violent riot.

Crowds immediately gathered to protest the officers' acquittals.

CHAPTER
SIX

RIOTS ERUPT

T he news of the Simi Valley trial verdict quickly swept the nation. Public figures and celebrities responded by announcing their shock to the media. Mayor Bradley responded by saying, "Today, the jury told the world that what we all saw with our own eyes was not a crime."[1] The public was already angry and upset about the trial's verdict. The officials' pronouncements added to the general feeling of disbelief and anger.

On April 29, 1992, within 62 minutes of the jury's verdict, the first related acts of violence began. Five African Americans entered a Korean-owned shop and stole bottles of alcohol. When the store owner's son tried to stop them, one youth hit him over the head with a bottle and shouted, "This is for Rodney King!"[2] Los Angeles was about to devolve into one of the biggest riots in American history.

By the early evening, a full-blown riot had taken over Los Angeles. Many of the rioters were African

A wave of violence swept the city the afternoon and evening of April 29, 1992.

Americans who were angry about the verdict. However, the majority of people who were arrested during the riots were Latino. Ultimately, rioters of many races participated. Angry people armed with baseball bats, rocks, and guns destroyed cars and set fires. One of the largest problems during the riots was looting. Many people in the area were poor and frustrated by their financial problems. They took advantage of the lawless state of the city to steal things they wanted and needed that they could not afford. The high rate of looting showed the riots were not just a response to the racial tensions between the white LAPD and oppressed minorities. They were also an angry response to years of financial stress.

Looters took advantage of the loss of order in the city.

The LAPD Retreats

The police were totally unprepared for the scale of the violence. They had no choice but to retreat to regroup and prepare themselves to handle the situation. Many neighborhoods of Los Angeles were left largely to the rioters. The main targets of the first day of the riots included white motorists, liquor stores, fast-food restaurants, and convenience stores.

While the violence and damage was widespread throughout the city, rioters converged in several key South Central locations to inflict damage. One area was the neighborhood surrounding the intersection of Florence and Normandie Avenues. This neighborhood would become one of the most violent and dangerous during the riots. A gang-led mob terrorized this area, attacking whites, Latinos, and Asians. The police pullout had left this high-crime area especially prone to chaos. Many people felt the LAPD should have shut down the streets and prevented traffic from passing through. An observer in a news helicopter remarked, "And there's no police presence down here! . . . This is attempted murder! Tell LAPD to shut [Florence] down, and Normandie!"[4]

A City Engulfed in Chaos

Another key area was near the Parker Center, the headquarters of the LAPD. The Parker Center represented the LAPD to many city residents, and it was

PEACEFUL PROTESTERS

Many L.A. residents who took to the streets after the verdict were peaceful protesters. Crowds of white, Asian, Latino, and African-American people gathered near the Simi Valley courthouse, the Parker Center, and other important L.A. landmarks to peacefully voice their frustrations. These nonviolent demonstrators held signs and posters and sang songs and chanted slogans, such as "The justice is for the other man, not for the brother man!" and "Justice for Rodney!"[5]

News reporters focused most of their attention on the violent rioters instead of on the nonviolent protests. Because of this, many people thought all of the protests after the verdict were violent. This was far from the truth.

Not all protesters used violence to make themselves heard.

one of the first locations peaceful protesters gathered
outside. They carried signs and called for justice for
Rodney King.

Soon, however, a small group of angry rioters
swarmed the scene. By about 6:40 p.m., a crowd of
rioters rushed the center and began throwing rocks and
bottles at the glass doors at the front of the building.
Soon the crowd pushed over a guard stand near the
parking lot and set it on fire.

Tensions between African Americans and Korean
Americans came to a head as the riot escalated. Many

of the stores and shops targeted during the riot were Korean owned. The Korean-American shop owners did anything they could to protect their stores, even wielding guns or knives against the looters.

Many people were quick to criticize the slow response of the LAPD. A major target was Chief Gates. When he was informed of the escalating violence in the city, he was attending a political fund-raiser in the wealthy Brentwood community. Rather than leaving the event to join the efforts to stop the violence, he stayed. Many people felt it showed Gates would rather enjoy a fancy event than fight crime in his own community.

The Beating of Reginald Denny

One of the most famous incidents that occurred on the first day of the riots was the attack on Reginald Denny. Denny, a white truck driver, was stopped at an intersection in the rioting Florence and Normandie neighborhood when a group of African Americans pulled him from the cab of his truck and onto the street. A hovering news helicopter filmed as an angry crowd severely beat Denny. One attacker used a concrete block to crush Denny's skull, fracturing it in 91 places and causing brain damage.[6] This attacker then celebrated as Denny bled on the ground. Luckily for Denny, four African-American neighborhood residents witnessed the attack on television and drove to the intersection. They waved the attackers off and drove Denny to a hospital, where he was treated for his critical injuries.

By the end of the first day of riots, people around the world were calling Los Angeles a "war zone."[7] Residents cowered in fear as news stations reported at least ten people had been killed in the violence, and more than 140 had been wounded. The LAPD's initial retreat made it seem as though rioters were taking over the city. Chief Gates incited even more anger by calling the looters and arsonists "gang members and drunks who were just waiting on an opportunity."[8] Law enforcement, media, and residents of Los Angeles wondered what would happen next, and who—if anyone—would come to the city's aid.

THE ATTACKERS

The world watched footage of Reginald Denny's assault in horror. The news helicopter that filmed the incident clearly captured the faces of the attackers.

However, when the three men were put on trial for their attack on Denny, many people felt they did not receive the punishment they deserved. One assailant was convicted of robbery and assault. The two others were convicted of smaller charges, a felony count of mayhem for one and a count of misdemeanor assault for the other.

CHAPTER
SEVEN

"CAN WE ALL GET ALONG?"

O n April 30, 1992, the second day of rioting, the situation in Los Angeles seemed even more precarious. Rioters appeared to grow more organized, targeting specific stores and areas. Store owners, especially Korean Americans, grew more and more defensive of their property, sometimes even engaging in gun battles with the rioters. It seemed as though Los Angeles could not sink any further into chaos.

Later that day, Mayor Bradley declared a state of emergency in the city. This meant the duties of all law enforcement officials shifted to preserving the peace in the city and protecting its citizens, rather than performing tasks such as traffic management or administration. The citizens of Los Angeles were warned to be especially cautious. Bradley also instituted a mandatory curfew for the whole city. From dusk until

An armed Korean man watched for looters from the roof of an L.A. store on April 30, 1992.

RIOTING NATIONWIDE

Los Angeles was not the only city plagued by rioting in the wake of the King verdict. Shortly after news of the acquittal of the four LAPD officers hit the airwaves, rioting erupted in San Francisco, California; Atlanta, Georgia; Chicago, Illinois; Oakland, California; Seattle, Washington; and Las Vegas, Nevada. Other cities, such as Baton Rouge, Louisiana, and Kansas City, Missouri, were home to organized, peaceful protests. Nationwide, law enforcement officers and government officials worked to increase security and discourage public organization. They did not want to face the large-scale violence that was destroying parts of Los Angeles.

dawn, no pedestrians or vehicles were permitted in public streets or areas. This rule was intended to keep both rioters and potential victims of riot violence safe. However, it had little effect. The violence in the city raged on. President George H. W. Bush weighed in, giving a speech from the Oval Office. He warned the rioters in Los Angeles their "anarchy" would not be tolerated.[1]

As the second day wound down, L.A. residents still complained the LAPD had not responded appropriately. Violence, rather than law, still ruled the streets. The LAPD was scrambling to respond to the huge influx of violent crime, theft, and arson, but it needed reinforcements. Many people realized the LAPD had been poorly prepared for any riots, much less one of this magnitude.

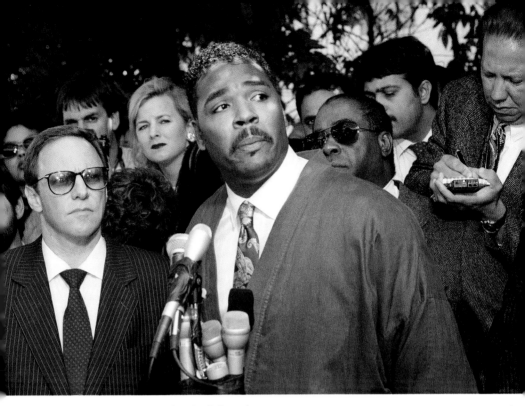

On May 1, 1992, the third day of rioting, King called for an end to the violence.

This revelation made some people only angrier with the police.

King Speaks

The third day of rioting finally brought the response the city needed. On that day, President Bush ordered military troops and riot-trained federal officers into the city. This action showed the residents of Los Angeles the country was indeed watching the events and help would soon arrive. Later that day, King joined in the efforts to calm the city. He made a public appearance in which he asked his fellow Angelenos, "People, I just want to say, can we all get along? Can we get along?"[2] These words would become a famous representation of the desperation felt by Los Angeles residents during these terrifying days.

By the fourth day of the riots, President Bush's military response had finally surged into the city. More than 10,000 National Guard and federal troops were hard at work restoring order to the city, block by block.[3] However, violent pockets still existed, and the work of law enforcement officials was still dangerous.

Order Is Restored

By May 4, the city was beginning to calm down. Law enforcement was restoring order, and residents began taking stock of the damage. Mayor Bradley lifted the curfew, again allowing pedestrians and vehicles out on the streets in the city. Shocked homeowners and business owners surveyed the destruction with sadness and disbelief. Many wondered how an event so disastrous could have occurred in the United States. They also wondered why help had not arrived sooner.

People around the world looked for someone to blame for the riots. The LAPD, whose public image had already suffered during the King trial, was a target for many people. Chief Gates defended the work of the LAPD but blamed some commanders for not deploying officers quickly enough into the hardest hit areas of South Central.

It became clear Los Angeles had just been the site of one of the country's most devastating riots. The numbers were staggering. Seven thousand fires had been reported. More than 12,000 people were arrested. Approximately $1 billion of property damage had occurred. More than 2,000 people had been injured.[4] And, shockingly, more than 50 people had been killed.[5]

Racial Rioting

At the beginning of the riots, the majority of rioters were African American, while the

THE MEDIA PLAYS A PART

Television and newspaper reporters gave huge amounts of attention to the looting taking place during the riots. Local viewers were bombarded with images of thousands of people breaking into stores and stealing goods including shoes, televisions, and groceries. Some people felt the news coverage of the looters actually encouraged bystanders to participate. Resident Vanessa Coleman remembers watching the news coverage of the looting and thinking, "Well, I better get out there and get stuff for my kids, too. . . . We didn't know if there were going to be any stores standing. We didn't know if we were going to have food."[6] She then joined a few friends and looted a nearby store.

victims of violence were white, Latino, and Asian. For African Americans, the King assault and trial seemed to follow a long chain of offenses that included slavery, lynchings, and racist police brutality. Some African Americans searching for a way to voice their frustrations and sadness over their continued racial oppression took to the streets and rioted.

However, as the riots progressed and the police presence continued to be minimal, much of the rioting began to turn into what historians have recognized as a diverse, multiethnic, "massive looting spree."[7] Many races participated in the looting, but Latino residents figured most predominantly. Latinos made up nearly half of the population of South Central at the time of the riots. Many were very poor. They targeted grocery stores and stole necessities, such as food and diapers.

It took the National Guard to help end the violent riots.

The Korean-American role in the riots was complex. They suffered more than any other racial group in the damages from the riots, with more than 2,000 Korean-American businesses destroyed and $400 million in damages.[9] However, some Korean-American business owners were seen as contributing to the violence in Los Angeles. They felt they were not protected by the LAPD. They used guns and knives to protect their stores and property. An image of two Korean shopkeepers firing guns at an advancing crowd of looters was played often on television. The *New York Times* saw the significance of it, noting, "The image seemed to speak of race war."[10] Americans were realizing the riots were not just about King. Rather, they were the response to

THE SHOW GOES ON

L.A. talk show host Arsenio Hall remembered working during the riots. Instead of canceling his show during the violence, he said he "fought hard to make sure we filmed no matter what. I felt I had a responsibility to . . . give those who weren't in Los Angeles a glimpse of ground zero." He donned a bulletproof vest and gave out food outside a church in South Central. His white friend Ron Burkle helped. Hall remembered, "People thought I was crazy taking a white guy straight into the heart of south central Los Angeles and into the center of a race riot." But Hall felt strongly about it. He said, "It was good to have a voice back then that could discuss every issue happening around the country to all people, but particularly for people of color."[11] His reporting helped Americans relate to the fear and chaos that was overtaking the city.

many racial, economic, and social tensions that had been brewing in Los Angeles for too long.

By May 9, the situation in the city was controlled enough for the federal troops and the National Guard to leave the city. It was once again up to the LAPD to maintain order. Store owners, residents, and lawmakers began thinking about how they would rebuild the city. They also wondered how to remedy the issues that had contributed to the riots in the first place. It was clear inequalities between races and different economic classes had grown too great. L.A. residents felt as though they were at war with one another. Somehow, the city would have to learn to heal.

CHAPTER
EIGHT

A FEDERAL TRIAL

In the midst of the Los Angeles riots, federal prosecutors started working on a second trial for the four LAPD officers who had been acquitted. President Bush had noted the result of the first trial had "left us all with a deep sense of personal frustration and anguish."[1] Americans were not satisfied with the result of the first trial. Many people felt as though the LAPD officers needed to be punished for their actions. This trial would take a slightly different approach from the Simi Valley trial. It would focus on whether the LAPD officers had violated King's civil rights during his arrest.

On August 4, 1992, a grand jury indicted three of the LAPD officers for "willfully and intentionally using unreasonable force." They also indicted Koon for "willfully permitting and failing to take action to stop the unlawful assault" on King.[2] Many civil rights leaders celebrated this news. They hoped the results of the trial would bring about punishment for the LAPD

King appeared in court during the second trial, which asked whether the police had violated his civil rights.

79

officers involved. They also hoped it would calm the still-angry public.

Different Strategies for the Federal Trial

The federal trial began on February 25, 1993, in Los Angeles County. Unlike the Simi Valley trial, this trial had a racially diverse jury, including two African Americans among its 12 members. Both the defense and

DOUBLE JEOPARDY

The Bill of Rights includes a special statement about a phenomenon called double jeopardy: "Nor shall any person be subject for the same offense to be twice put in jeopardy of life or limb." This means no US citizen can be tried for the same crime twice. This law was created to protect the innocent from being subjected to long, repeated trials. It was also intended to ensure trials achieved the best possible results.

King's federal trial charged the four LAPD officers with essentially the same conduct as the Simi Valley trial: using excessive force against a suspected criminal. Many people wondered if the officers could avoid the second trial by claiming it would be a case of double jeopardy.

The federal case was allowed to proceed because it did not charge the LAPD officers with the exact same crimes as the Simi Valley trial. It focused on the violation of King's civil rights. It also charged the officers with the "intent to inflict on-the-scene punishment without due process of law."[3] These differences were enough to justify a second trial.

prosecution teams were prepared for a difficult trial. They had seen the results of the Simi Valley trial and were aware the results of this trial could result in public anger and even riots. Both sides of the trial also carefully studied the Simi Valley trial and selected witnesses according to their success or failure the first time they testified.

One of the biggest differences between the Simi Valley trial and the federal trial was that King testified in the second trial. He had been purposefully prevented from testifying at the first trial because prosecutors feared he could turn the jury against him to favor the defendants instead. In the federal trial, however, prosecutors knew he could be an asset.

King's testimony had a dramatic effect on the jury. In the Simi Valley trial, prosecutors feared he would come across as an angry criminal. The federal trial proved they were wrong. Instead of hurting his case, as the first prosecution team had feared, he came across as an honest witness. Many witnesses reflected he appeared to be a genuine, though uneducated and confused, man. King even seemed unsure whether race was a motivator in his attack. He testified that as he was being beaten, the officers were either saying, "What's up killer? How do you feel killer?" or "What's up nigger?" When King was asked to clarify which term was used, he replied, "I'm not sure."[4] His humble attitude had a strong effect on the jury. He did not seem like a violent and unstable person who would need to be subdued by the police.

The prosecution also focused on the injuries King sustained during his attack. A medical expert witness claimed King's facial injuries were caused by a police baton, not by being thrown to the ground, as the LAPD officers had claimed. This testimony emphasized the force and extent of King's beating. It also cast doubt on the LAPD officers for denying they had caused this injury.

The prosecution tried hard to make the LAPD officers seem untrustworthy. They suggested to the jury the expert witnesses and LAPD officers who testified on behalf of the defense were simply friends trying to bail their buddies out of a tight spot. This was very

Briseno, *left*, and his lawyer, *right*, speaking to the media during the federal trial, with Koon in the background

successful. The prosecution made the defense appear as though they were a gang of bullies.

The team of lawyers defending the LAPD officers used a very different strategy for the federal trial than it had used in the Simi Valley trial. It did not focus on Koon's fears or doubts during the attack. This made it seem as though he was arrogant and aloof. Instead, Koon spent his time on the stand defending the level of force his team had used on King. Officer Powell's lawyers were afraid the prosecution would attack his character. They kept him from testifying at all. They knew how much damage his "gorillas in the mist" comment had done during the Simi Valley trial and were

BRISENO'S VIDEOTAPE

Officer Briseno's lawyer did not want him to testify in the federal case. He was afraid Briseno would be associated with the negative characterizations of Koon and Powell. Instead, he allowed Briseno to appear in court as a witness in a heavily edited videotape. This decision proved harmful for the LAPD officers on trial. Briseno could not defend himself or answer questions about the statements he made in the video. Instead, the video ended up being used by the prosecution as more evidence of the problems with the LAPD's actions. Ultimately, Briseno was acquitted along with Officer Wind. The jury found Briseno and Wind had not violated King's civil rights by using excessive force.

afraid of what could happen in this trial. Officer Wind also decided not to testify. His role in the video had already created huge problems in his life. He wanted to keep a low profile. Officer Briseno did appear as a witness, but only via a videotape presented in the courtroom.

Before the jury began deliberations, one of the defense lawyers told the jury he understood how much pressure they were under. He said, "No man should be condemned in this country because there is a threat of riot. So in a sense, my client is on trial, but you are also on trial; it's your courage that's on trial."[5] He was encouraging the jury to think about the facts of the trial, not the possible public outcry if they made an unpopular decision.

A Verdict Is Announced

After six days of deliberation, the jury members made up their minds on April 16. However, the judge delayed the announcement of the verdict until the following morning to reduce the risk of riots. At 7:00 a.m. the following morning, the court announced two of the officers, Koon and Powell, had been found guilty. Both Koon and Powell were sentenced to 30 months in federal correctional camps. Officers Wind and Briseno were acquitted.

Upon hearing the news, the city of Los Angeles remained calm and in a state of order. No violence or looting followed the announcement. City officials and law enforcement breathed a sigh of relief. It seemed as though the city would remain peaceful. However, it was clear there were many issues that needed to be addressed to prevent further unrest.

THE JURY DELIBERATES

Tensions were high as the jury deliberated its decision. Over six days, they swung from favoring acquittal to eventually deciding Koon and Powell were guilty. There were heated arguments, and some jurors even reported name-calling. After one particularly angry exchange, a juror even ran from the deliberation room crying. When the final decision was reached, the jurors seemed to have unified. They even high-fived as they agreed on their final decision.

CHAPTER
NINE

RODNEY KING'S LEGACY

In the aftermath of the King beating and subsequent trials, the city of Los Angeles was physically scarred. The fires, looting, and vandalism that had occurred during the six days of rioting left some South Central neighborhoods almost unrecognizable. To begin repairing the city, Mayor Bradley started a program called Rebuild L.A. It promised to bring in money over the course of five years to replace the structures that were destroyed. However, Rebuild L.A. promised more than it could deliver. It accomplished little and was largely considered a failure.

In June 1992, the LAPD saw a momentous change. Gates resigned from his position as chief of police. He had held this role for 14 years. After the riots ended, many residents were angry about how he handled the police response. The media blamed him for the destruction that occurred in the city. Minority

After the riots, shop owners and L.A. residents had to clean up the damage.

communities also distrusted and disliked him because of racially insensitive comments he made throughout his tenure. He was sad to leave, but he worried the attention he was getting was hurting the effectiveness of the police force.

In the wake of the failed efforts of Rebuild L.A., many small businesses left the city. The damages they had sustained, or witnessed other businesses sustain, made the area seem too dangerous. Shopkeepers did not want to risk staying in the city during another riot.

COMPENSATION FOR KING

In 1994, King took the city of Los Angeles to a civil trial seeking financial compensation. The city accepted liability for his beating and offered to pay him $1.25 million. However, King wanted much more, $9.5 million.

On April 20, 1994, the trial ended. The city of Los Angeles was ordered to pay King $3.8 million in damages.[1] King used the money to pay for his extensive medical bills, which covered the broken bones and neurological and psychological damage he suffered after his beating.

He also used the money to pay his legal expenses, which included hundreds of thousands of dollars owed to his lawyers. King's lawyers noted he would never be able to work again, so the financial reward would also help him pay for basic living expenses.

After the verdict from this civil trial was announced, some city leaders feared another riot could occur. However, the streets of Los Angeles remained calm. It seemed as though many people were glad to see King would be receiving payment from the city.

Many longtime residents chose to leave the area as well. African Americans moved out in large numbers. Between 1992 and 2007, 123,000 African Americans moved to other cities. South Los Angeles, an area that was once predominantly African American, is now very different. Latino residents make up 54 percent of its population, and African Americans represent only 42 percent.[2] This change in racial diversity can be attributed to fears that followed the riots. But it is also a product of the continued economic and social struggle faced by minorities in Los Angeles. Jobs are still difficult to find in the area, and the cost of living is still very high.

Residents all over the city were emotionally scarred. They lived in fear another riot would break out. It was clear the police, government, and citizens of Los Angeles needed to make major changes in order to repair the physical and mental state of the city. A national survey taken by the *New York Times* in the aftermath of the riots showed the country was in a "shaken, worried mood," and citizens were "more likely to see the unrest as a symptom of festering social needs than as a simple issue of law and order."[3] They did not think of the riots solely as an angry response to the brutality of the police.

Racism remained an issue in Los Angeles and the United States as a whole in the wake of the riots.

They knew the days of violence were also a large-scale reaction to prolonged poverty and discrimination faced by minorities in the area.

Racial tensions in Los Angeles and around the country were clearly in need of repair. The *New York Times* survey also showed 75 percent of African Americans and 67 percent of whites felt race relations in the United States were "generally bad." And more than 50 percent of both whites and African Americans in the survey predicted there would still be race riots in US cities 25 years in the future.[4] These bleak reports showed Americans there was much work to do to improve interracial interaction and racial disparities in employment, income, education, and other areas in the future.

A Time for Change

Some historians have looked to the Los Angeles riots as a series of events that gave a voice to a population that had long been ignored. The poor, uneducated, and minority residents of South Central had struggled for years to find safe housing, good jobs, and equal treatment. Though the riots that followed the King verdict physically devastated many areas of the city, they also made it impossible for the media and mainstream America to ignore the discrimination and unfair treatment these people had long endured. The riots gave a voice to the oppressed Angelenos.

In the years since the riots, much work has been done to improve race relations in Los Angeles and around the country. A survey taken in 2012 showed 70 percent of Los Angeles residents feel as though race relations have improved since the riots.[5] However, many people feel as though there is still much work to do. Noted *LA Weekly* journalist Erin Aubry Kaplan

KING'S AUTOBIOGRAPHY

In 2012, King published an autobiography titled *The Riot Within: My Journey from Rebellion to Redemption.* In it, he wrote optimistically about his hopes: "We may be scarred . . . and we may not be able to forget, but we can keep going, one step at a time, until we get to a better place."[7] King genuinely hoped for a better, brighter future for all Americans, regardless of their race.

commented on the progress of American race relations: "We talk about Latinos, immigrants, gays, but we don't talk nearly enough about black people as a whole. . . . African-Americans are becoming less and less visible."[6] Achieving better race relations is an ongoing mission of many city leaders and activists. The Los Angeles riots showed Americans how fragile a society can be if race relations are allowed to grow too tense or troubled.

King left a deep impression on American law enforcement officials and civilians alike. In 2012, African-American teenager Trayvon Martin was shot and killed by a man who felt as though the teen was acting in a threatening manner. But many people believed Martin had been racially profiled. When George Zimmerman, the man who shot Martin, was found not guilty of murder or manslaughter, many Americans were reminded of the Rodney King Simi Valley trial. After the Zimmerman verdict was announced, many cities even prepared for riots similar to those that followed the King verdict announcement. Although the verdict was protested in dozens of cities across the nation, rioting of the magnitude that consumed Los Angeles in 1992 did not occur.

King's Later Life

As the city of Los Angeles worked to rebuild its social order and physical structures, King struggled to stay on the right side of the law. He was arrested multiple times for drunk driving and spousal abuse. He was also accused of attacking an undercover police officer.

King continued battling substance abuse problems. He even appeared on the television show *Celebrity Rehab with Dr. Drew* in 2008 to address his ongoing alcoholism, but he was unable to conquer his addictions. On June 17, 2012, his fiancée Cynthia Kelley found him dead in his swimming pool at his Rialto, California, home. He had accidentally drowned after drinking alcohol and doing drugs. King was 47 when he died.

Rodney King did not think of himself as an American hero. He was simply a man whose assault ignited anger in a city that was already buckling under racial, social, political, and economic stress. He will be remembered for the pain he endured at the hands of the LAPD, and for his famous plea: "Can we all get along?"

King's legacy is his desire for peace and understanding.

TIMELINE

1965
Rodney King is born in Sacramento, California, on April 4.

1965
Riots rage in the Watts neighborhood of Los Angeles, California, in August.

1988
Operation Hammer, the attempt by the Los Angeles Police Department (LAPD) to crack down on gang violence, begins in April.

1988
LAPD troops raid an apartment complex at Thirty-Ninth Street and Dalton Avenue on August 1.

1989
King is arrested for robbing a convenience store with a tire iron on November 3.

1991

King is assaulted by LAPD officers while George Holliday films from his balcony on March 3.

1991

Holliday brings his videotape to Los Angeles news station KTLA on March 4.

1991

King is released from police custody without charges on March 6.

1991

A Los Angeles grand jury indicts Sergeant Stacy Koon and Officers Laurence Powell, Timothy Wind, and Theodore Briseno on March 14.

1991

Korean-American store owner Soon Ja Du kills African-American Latasha Harlins on March 16.

1991

Superior Court judge Stanley Weisberg moves the Rodney King beating trial from Los Angeles to nearby Simi Valley on November 26.

TIMELINE

1992
The Simi Valley trial begins on March 5.

1992
All four LAPD officers are acquitted of using excessive force on April 29. Later that day, riots start in South Central L.A., and Reginald Denny is assaulted.

1992
Riots rage on in Los Angeles from April 30 to May 4.

1992
Federal troops are removed from the city on May 9 and order is restored in Los Angeles.

1992
In June, Daryl Gates resigns as LAPD chief of police after 14 years of service.

1992

A federal grand jury indicts Koon, Powell, Wind, and Briseno on charges of violating King's civil rights on August 4.

1993

The federal Rodney King beating trial begins on February 25.

1993

A federal jury convicts Koon and Powell on charges of violating King's civil rights. Wind and Briseno are found not guilty on April 16. The verdict is announced on April 17.

1994

King is awarded $3.8 million in damages from a civil lawsuit against the city of Los Angeles in April.

2012

King is found dead in his home in Rialto, California, on June 17. He is 47.

ESSENTIAL FACTS

Date of Event
1991–1992

Place of Event
Los Angeles, California

Key Players
- Rodney King

- Sergeant Stacey Koon

- Officer Laurence Powell

- Officer Timothy Wind

- Officer Theodore Briseno

- Officer Rolando Solano

- George Holliday

- LAPD chief Daryl Gates

Highlights of Event

- Rodney King resisted arrest after being pulled over under suspicion of driving under the influence of alcohol. He was repeatedly kicked and struck by members of the LAPD, resulting in serious injuries. The incident was filmed and the video was shown worldwide.

- The LAPD officers involved in King's arrest were put on trial for using excessive force. A jury with no African Americans acquitted all four LAPD officers.

- The city of LA reacted to the verdict of the Simi Valley trial with a six-day riot. More than 12,000 people were arrested, more than 2,000 people were injured, more than 50 people were killed, and $1 billion in damages was sustained by the city of Los Angeles.

- A federal trial was held to determine if the LAPD officers had violated King's civil rights. The jury returned guilty verdicts for Sergeant Koon and Officer Powell. Officers Wind and Briseno were acquitted.

Quote

"People, I just want to say, can we all get along? Can we get along?"—*Rodney King*

GLOSSARY

defense
The case presented by, or on behalf of, a person defending himself or herself in a court of law.

discrimination
Unfair treatment based on a person's religion, race, or sex.

excessive force
Unnecessary amounts of force used to arrest or subdue a suspect.

indict
To formally accuse someone of something, usually in reference to legal proceedings.

Jehovah's Witness
A member of a religious group that preaches the Second Coming of Christ.

looting
Stealing things during a war, fire, or other disturbance.

lynch
To put to death by mob action for a perceived crime without giving the accused a trial.

parole
To release a prisoner from incarceration under the promise of good behavior.

probation
The release of a prisoner or offender subject to supervision.

prosecution
The case presented by, or on behalf of, a party bringing charges against another.

racial profiling
The unfair targeting of people of color by law enforcement or security organizations for investigation or scrutiny.

testify
To give evidence as part of a court proceeding.

verdict
The official decision made in a civil or criminal court case.

ADDITIONAL RESOURCES

Selected Bibliography

Cannon, Lou. *Official Negligence: How Rodney King and the Riots Changed Los Angeles and the LAPD.* New York: Random, 1999. Print.

King, Rodney. *The Riot Within: My Journey from Rebellion to Redemption.* New York: Harper, 2012. Print.

Linder, Douglas. "The Rodney King Beating Trials." *Jurist.* University of Pittsburgh School of Law, Dec. 2001. Web. 8 June 2013.

Ogletree, Charles J. *Beyond the Rodney King Story.* Lebanon, NH: Northeastern UP, 1994. Print.

Further Readings

McWhorter, Diane. *A Dream of Freedom.* New York: Scholastic, 2004. Print.

Takaki, Ronald, and Rebecca Stefoff, adapter. *A Different Mirror for Young People: A History of Multicultural America.* New York: Seven Stories, 2012. Print.

Web Sites

To learn more about Rodney King and the L.A. riots, visit ABDO Publishing Company online at **www.abdopublishing.com**. Web sites about Rodney King and the L.A. riots are featured on our Book Links page. These links are routinely monitored and updated to provide the most current information available.

Places to Visit

California African American Museum
600 State Drive
Los Angeles, CA 90037
213-744-7432
http://www.caamuseum.org
Visit this museum to learn about African-American history and culture in the state of California.

The Los Angeles Police Museum
6045 York Boulevard
Los Angeles, CA 90042
323-344-9445
http://www.laphs.org
Visit the Los Angeles Police Historical Society to learn more about this historic police department.

SOURCE NOTES

Chapter 1. The Arrest That Made History

1. Lou Cannon. *Official Negligence: How Rodney King and the Riots Changed Los Angeles and the LAPD.* New York: Random, 1999. Print. 25.

2. Ibid. 51.

3. Ibid. 31.

4. Seth Mydans. "Los Angeles Policemen Acquitted in Taped Beating." *New York Times.* New York Times, 29 Apr. 1992. Web. 23 Sept. 2013.

5. Jerome H. Skolnick and James J. Fyfe. *Above the Law: Police and the Excessive Use of Force.* New York: Simon, 1993. *Google Book Search.* Web. 23 Sept. 2013.

6. Lou Cannon. *Official Negligence: How Rodney King and the Riots Changed Los Angeles and the LAPD.* New York: Random, 1999. Print. 37–38.

7. Ibid. 38.

8. Ibid. 50.

9. Cathleen Decker. "The Times Poll: Most Rank Police High in L.A. and Orange Counties." *Los Angeles Times.* Los Angeles Times, 13 Feb. 1990. Web. 23 Sept. 2013.

Chapter 2. An Early Viral Video

1. Lou Cannon. *Official Negligence: How Rodney King and the Riots Changed Los Angeles and the LAPD.* New York: Random, 1999. Print. 22.

2. Ibid. 22.

3. Ibid. 22.

4. Ibid. 23.

5. Ibid. 21.

6. Ibid. 24.

7. Ibid. 24.

8. Ibid. 49.

9. Ibid. 49.

10. Ibid. 23.

11. Ibid. 25.

12. "The Legacy of Rodney King." *Frontline.* PBS: WGBH Educational Foundation, n.d. Web. 23 Sept. 2013.

13. Lou Cannon. *Official Negligence: How Rodney King and the Riots Changed Los Angeles and the LAPD.* New York: Random, 1999. Print. 49.

14. Ibid.

Chapter 3. Life in Los Angeles

1. Alejandra Lopez. "Demographics of California Counties: A Comparison of 1980, 1990, and 2000 Census Data." *Center for Comparative Studies in Race and Ethnicity.* Stanford University, 9 June 2002. Web. 23 Sept. 2013.

2. Lou Cannon. *Official Negligence: How Rodney King and the Riots Changed Los Angeles and the LAPD.* New York: Random, 1999. Print. 4.

3. Ibid. 8.

4. Ibid. 10.

5. Ibid. 15–16.

6. Patrick Range McDonald. "Then and Now: Images from the Same Spot as the L.A. Riots, 20 Years Later." *LA Weekly.* LA Weekly, n.d. Web. 23 Sept. 2013.

7. Ibid.

8. Edward T. Chang. "Korean American Community Coalesces." *Los Angeles Times.* Los Angeles Times, 29 April 2012. Web. 23 Sept. 2013.

9. Lou Cannon. *Official Negligence: How Rodney King and the Riots Changed Los Angeles and the LAPD.* New York: Random, 1999. Print. 17.

Chapter 4. Who Is Rodney King?

1. "Watts Riots." *Civil Rights Digital Library.* Digital Library of Georgia, 21 Aug. 2013. Web. 23 Sept. 2013.

2. Rodney King. *The Riot Within: My Journey from Rebellion to Redemption.* New York: Harper, 2012. Print. 4–5.

3. Ibid. 6.

4. Emily Langer. "Rodney King Dies." *Washington Post.* Washington Post, 17 June 2012. Web. 23 Sept. 2013.

5. Lou Cannon. *Official Negligence: How Rodney King and the Riots Changed Los Angeles and the LAPD.* New York: Random, 1999. Print. 42.

6. Michel Martin. "Rodney King's Personal Struggle with Alcohol." *NPR.* NPR, 20 June 2012. Web. 23 Sept. 2013.

7. Lou Cannon. *Official Negligence: How Rodney King and the Riots Changed Los Angeles and the LAPD.* New York: Random, 1999. Print. 43.

8. Gretchen Voss. "Rodney King's Daughters." *Glamour.* Condé Nast, Feb. 2011. Web. 23 Sept. 2013.

Chapter 5. The Simi Valley Trial

1. Douglas Linder. "The Trials of Los Angeles Police Officers in Connection with the Beating of Rodney King." *law2.umkc.edu.* University of Missouri–Kansas City, 2001. Web. 23 Sept. 2013.

2. Lou Cannon. *Official Negligence: How Rodney King and the Riots Changed Los Angeles and the LAPD.* New York: Random, 1999. Print. 181.

3. Ibid. 180.

4. Ibid. 181.

5. Ibid. 181.

6. Ibid. 187.

7. Ibid. 81.

SOURCE NOTES CONTINUED

8. Ibid. 77.

9. Douglas Linder. "The Trials of Los Angeles Police Officers in Connection with the Beating of Rodney King." *law2.umkc.edu.* University of Missouri–Kansas City, 2001. Web. 23 Sept. 2013.

10. Ibid.

11. Ibid.

12. Ibid.

Chapter 6. Riots Erupt

1. Douglas Linder. "The Trials of Los Angeles Police Officers in Connection with the Beating of Rodney King." *law2.umkc.edu.* University of Missouri–Kansas City, 2001. Web. 23 Sept. 2013.

2. Ibid.

3. Douglas Linder. "The Rodney King Beating Trials." *Jurist.* University of Pittsburgh School of Law, Dec. 2001. Web. 23 Sept. 2013.

4. Lou Cannon. *Official Negligence: How Rodney King and the Riots Changed Los Angeles and the LAPD.* New York: Random, 1999. Print. 303.

5. Leezel Tanglao. "Lost Angeles Riots 20 Years Later." *ABC News.* ABC News, 29 Apr. 2012. Web. 23 Sept. 2013.

6. Lou Cannon. *Official Negligence: How Rodney King and the Riots Changed Los Angeles and the LAPD.* New York: Random, 1999. Print. 308.

7. Playthell Benjamin. "From the Archive, 1 May 1992: Rodney King Verdict Sparks LA Riots." *Guardian.* Guardian, 1 May 2013. Web. 23 Sept. 2013.

8. Ibid.

Chapter 7. "Can We All Get Along?"

1. "Voices of the L.A. Riots." *Daily Beast.* Newsweek/Daily Beast, n.d. Web. 24 Sept. 2013.

2. Jennifer Medina. "Rodney King Dies at 47." *New York Times.* New York Times, 17 June 2012. Web. 24 Sept. 2013.

3. Allison Samuels. "How Did Rodney King Die?" *Daily Beast.* Newsweek/Daily Beast, 11 July 2012. Web. 24 Sept. 2013.

4. Melissa Palmer. "Los Angeles 1992 Riots: By the Numbers." *NBC Southern California.* NBC Universal, 20 Apr. 2012. Web. 24 Sept. 2013.

5. Marc Lacey. "Riot Death Toll Lowered to 51 after Coroner's Review." *Los Angeles Times.* Los Angeles Times, 12 Aug. 1992. Web. 24 Sept. 2013.

6. Lou Cannon. *Official Negligence: How Rodney King and the Riots Changed Los Angeles and the LAPD.* New York: Random, 1999. Print. 338.

7. Ibid. 337.

8. Gretchen Voss. "Rodney King's Daughters." *Glamour.* Condé Nast, Feb. 2011. Web. 23 Sept. 2013.

9. Lou Cannon. *Official Negligence: How Rodney King and the Riots Changed Los Angeles and the LAPD*. New York: Random, 1999. Print. 336.

10. Seth Mydans. "Riot in Los Angeles." *New York Times*. New York Times, 3 May 1992. Web. 24 Sept. 2013.

11. Arsenio Hall. "Arsenio Hall on Filming from L.A. Riots' Ground Zero." *Daily Beast*. Newsweek/Daily Beast, 26 Apr. 2012. Web. 24 Sept. 2013.

Chapter 8. A Federal Trial

1. Douglas Linder. "The Trials of Los Angeles Police Officers in Connection with the Beating of Rodney King." *law2.umkc.edu*. University of Missouri–Kansas City, 2001. Web. 23 Sept. 2013.

2. Ibid.

3. "It's Not Double Jeopardy In L.A." *New York Times*. New York Times, 8 Apr. 1993. Web. 24 Sept. 2013.

4. Douglas Linder. "The Trials of Los Angeles Police Officers in Connection with the Beating of Rodney King." *law2.umkc.edu*. University of Missouri–Kansas City, 2001. Web. 23 Sept. 2013.

5. Ibid.

Chapter 9. Rodney King's Legacy

1. Seth Mydans. "Rodney King Is Awarded $3.8 Million." *New York Times*. New York Times, 20 Apr. 1994. Web. 24 Sept. 2013.

2. Patrick Range McDonald. "Then and Now: Images from the Same Spot as the L.A. Riots, 20 Years Later." *LA Weekly*. LA Weekly, n.d. Web. 23 Sept. 2013.

3. Robin Toner. "After the Riots: Los Angeles Riots are a Warning, Americans Fear." *New York Times*. New York Times, 11 May 1992. Web. 24 Sept. 2013.

4. Ibid.

5. "Trayvon Who? Most Angelenos See Improved Race Relations Post-LA Riots." *CBS Los Angeles*. CBS Local Media, 12 Apr. 2012. Web. 24 Sept. 2013.

6. Dennison Giongco. "Panelists Discuss Effects of LA Riots on Race Relations." *Daily Trojan*. University of Southern California, 29 Apr. 2013. Web. 24 Sept. 2013.

7. Anthony McCartney and Raquel Maria Dillon, Associated Press. "Rev. Jesse Jackson Mourns the Death of Rodney King." *WBEZ 91.5*. Chicago Public Media, 18 June 2012. Web. 24 Sept. 2013.

8. Ibid.

9. Kate Mather. "Rev. Jesse Jackson says Rodney King 'Seemed to Be on a High Note." *Los Angeles Times*. Los Angeles Times, 17 June 2012. Web. 24 Sept. 2013.

INDEX

ABOUT THE AUTHOR

Rebecca Rissman is a nonfiction author and editor. She has written more than 200 books about history, science, and art. Her book *Shapes in Sports* earned a starred review from *Booklist*, and her series *Animal Spikes and Spines* received *Learning Magazine*'s 2013 Teachers Choice for Children's Books. She lives in Portland, Oregon, with her husband, and enjoys hiking, yoga, and cooking.

ABOUT THE CONSULTANT

Darnell Hunt is director of the Ralph J. Bunche Center for African American Studies and professor of sociology at UCLA. Dr. Hunt has written several scholarly books on the role of race in America, including *Screening the Los Angeles "Riots": Race, Seeing, and Resistance* (1997) and *Black Los Angeles: American Dreams and Racial Realities* (2010), coedited with Ana-Christina Ramon. He is a native of Washington, DC, who has lived in Los Angeles for more than 30 years.